I0782985

HOW DID I GET RICH?

AND WHAT DID I DO WITH THE MONEY?

BY BURAK CINAR

What to Expect in this Book?

Let me tell you a very simple secret. The world is a farm and there are some farmers. They are called the filthy rich. And we are the sheep. If we are not born as one of them, we will always be the sheep. But we can become a better sheep. There are some paths that lead us to become a better sheep, and you need to work on them to break your shackles. So, in this book, I will tell you about these paths and will guide you to your success on becoming a better sheep, just like I did...

And how did I get rich? That's the ultimate question, isn't it? Well, for the answer, let me say this first that it was not a lottery. It was not Bitcoin or any other coins either, or also wasn't heritage. It was only my ideas, my projects, hard thinking, hard work and patience in the end. Now I will not do some word tricks and will not start by using long psychological phrases like what is money or why do we need money, but instead, will go into the subjects directly. I wrote this book in a personal development style such as a step-by-step guide and made it to let you learn what I have been through. I did everything with zero budget, so yes, it is hard to digest this but, believe it or not, the only budget was merely my time; and by doing that, I managed to be successful enough to cover my, and my whole family's expenses, and saved enough for not to work anymore in my entire life and still adding more in the pot for my future generations...

Let me say that I wrote my real experiences about what I did in every detail and included my future projects in this book, and I will make sure that by following my steps, you will find your active or passive income in some ways, as I did. Trust me, everything you find in this book has been tried by me. No fake information and no scam, and I will not ask anything back from you but your good thoughts.

So, enough talk, time is money! Here is some stuff that you are going to find in this book and let me start by giving you some headlines. Firstly, as you can see, an e-book with full details of publishing which provides the best passive income. Secondly, writing articles on any subject that pays you in some ways. Thirdly, designing book covers such as this one and creating NFTs with creating wallets. And a Facebook group or a page that works on ads. Then, a wisely created Spotify Channel that gives you royalties. And the big one that is not passive but gives you a big boost, which is called referring people to jobs. And lastly, a very basic YouTube Channel and promising Instagram accounts with web pages that support each other. Each of them needs serious and massive work, but when all done, you will only need to worry about where to spend all the money. These are not all, you will also find some other bits that work, but are not too big, such as selling game accounts and trading game items, reviewing places, reviewing items, or reviewing anything on some platforms. Also, some upcoming projects that will shine when they are completed.

And do not miss the fun part, spending all the money! I am not a big spender, because small things make me happy, but when I do, I do things that I really enjoy. This is not the main idea of this book, but you will find a small section of what I did with the money and what I have been doing with it. Don't get jealous, and don't be a hater as this book will be your guide to achieve your dreams and will be the lead to take you out of the modern-slave life, and will free you.

Special Part just for the "Haters" before I start:

You must have heard this saying: "Haters gonna hate!"

I am sure all the haters are now seeking these answers but no...

They are all like "please be lottery, please be lottery!"

But no, I did not win a lottery.

Then Bitcoin? No, not crypto either!

Heritage? No!

And now they are like "please say you lost it all, please lose it all!"

But no, I did not lose any of it, in fact, I am putting more on. Why would I lose them all anyway? Is this what you would expect from me? Hah never!

So, as a summary again for haters, repeat this at the same time but loudly:

How did I get rich?

Not with a lottery!

What did I do with the money?

Did not lose any of it and still adding it up!

Keep saying this until your hearts full of hatred gets tired...

And I shall add:

How did I write this book?

With pleasure!

Haters can leave now!

Contents

So It Begins...

Shall I give you another secret? Well, it is not a secret if you are very well aware of what's going on in this clown world but let me ask you some questions.

A very basic one, do you know why you are going to school? Or why you went to school? Or why do you go to work? Why, why, why? Similar questions... The answer is easy: Because of rich people.

How come? First of all, let me say that I am not in that richest category. Anyway, the reason of this answer above is, there is a system that richest people own the world, and we are adapting to their system. Sorry but if you can't see that, you must be living your own pink fake world without knowing everything. Maybe it is good, what do they say, ignorance is bliss.

Do you think scientists cannot create a very simple light bulb that can go over hundred years? They can, but they don't. Why? For the economy. They make a bulb that goes about six months, and the system want you to spend your money. This is one of the very simple examples.

Coming with numbers from Wikipedia now: "...half of the world's net wealth belongs to the top 1%, top 10% of adults hold 85%, while the bottom 90% hold the remaining 15% of the world's total wealth, top 30% of adults hold 97% of the total wealth..."

If you are not in that richest people category, you are in that system. You need to go to school, you need to go to work. That is your life. You live for the rich people. You live so the system can feed the rich. You live to pay your taxes and bills. You need to do this so the rich people can do whatever they want. And there is only one thing that they are afraid of: Change of the system.

However, the system will never change, so at the conclusion, there are a few hundreds of rich people in the world, and we are all living for them. Yes, read it again, we live for them.

Was that a good summary? Truth hurts, doesn't it? Anyway, you must be thinking if I am in that richest people class but no. I am not and I will not and I cannot. But I will give you numbers that I earn, I know you really want to learn it and I will not keep it hidden.

As for me, being rich is about being rich in heart. But for wealth, it means to me that if you can do whatever you want in your life, then you are wealthy. And if you are not a slave of the system which I just described above, you are rich and wealthy. In order to do that, you need to have savings and passive income, you will never need to work, and you can give enough for your family.

So, again with numbers, I know you really need to see it this way so what I am saying can make more sense. I will give examples from England, the country I am living in.

Do you know the least amount of income that one can earn in England? It changes but let's say, they work for £10 per hour. It is only allowed to do 37.5 hours per week. In total this makes them earn £1.500,00 per month.

There are still jobs that pays £8 per hour but on average let's say £1.5K.

Another job for a person with a degree and certification can make them earn about £2.5K. But to earn that, they work full time which means 5 days of working in front of a computer or with people around. Well, £2.5K is good money in England, the power of the pound is the best so with this money, you can live well. But it wouldn't be enough. Because half of it went to the rent or mortgage, leaving you one thousand cash to spend or save each month.

But then why are we saving the money? For what? Let's say, you made 100.000 pounds by saving it for 10 years. You didn't eat, sleep, you haven't had a holiday; but you made 100K cash. Okay, well done, but what will you do with the money? You will probably buy a house but with the 100K extra cash, the house you will buy will have 4 rooms, instead of 3. So, in the end, you wasted your 10 years of life for that 1 extra room... Now this is painful, isn't it?

This is actually the main idea of the book. Think again, you didn't spend your valuable 10 years with your family, you didn't buy something small that you wanted, you didn't do anything, and for what? For that one extra room in your house? Did it really worth it? Does it worth really not to do something for 10 years just for another room? Really? And you know what? Most of the people do that but they are not aware of it. Some of them find it when their time is coming to end, but then all left is wishes, and regrets... Sorry but there is no going back, what's done is done, you did this choice, you wanted to waste your life of 10 years for that room.

Same goes for other examples, you didn't do anything for your life, but you slaved yourself and saved some cash and instead of a small car, you bought a big car. Again, you wasted your life for the size of the car.

Sorry again, but if you are not spending your money for your leisure and your pleasure, you are not living your life. You should live it, believe me, spend everything for yourself and for your family aka the loved ones. Another extra room will not bring you happiness, but a small family time dinner will be priceless.

I watched so many people, spending their lives for nothing. If you give them 1000 years of life, they will keep doing the same. Could we be living in a simulation? This brings the funny question, doesn't it? Anyway, although this is something that I think about, this is not what I will talk about.

Watching these desperate, hopeless people and getting annoyed by being a slave and because of my rebellious and stubborn personality kicked me one day and I said to myself that I will not be a part of this system! I said, I have only one life, one family and I will never be a slave! I said freedom. And I wanted it and I got it!

I promised to give you numbers, so here they are: My passive income is about between 5K and 10K each month. It changes every time, there is no payroll, so I give you only the average. And I earn it by doing literally nothing! All is coming in by royalties. Well, I worked, I am not saying I did nothing. I published four English books and some Turkish books, this will be the fifth one, and lots of draft works, I really forgot how many. Turkish books didn't bring much but having four books on Amazon roughly gives around 3K or 4K every month. It changes, but I am talking about the average. The rest comes from YouTube, articles, and other bits.

Believe me, with this number, I can do whatever I want! And I do! But mostly I spend it for quality family time. This is the most important thing for me. As I said, I am rich in heart. I don't need 10 houses, each of them would be a trouble and would keep me apart from family. If I can eat and drink and have some happy and peaceful time with my family, and not worry about their future, this will be the only thing that makes me feel great.

You had enough, didn't you? And do you still want to learn more? Or do you want to get one idea and start earning for your passive income? Then please carry on to the subjects. I am sure one of them will be suitable and when you see yourself successful on one of them, you will keep doing more and free yourself from the system like me.

So, let me say it again in a summary: It is no lottery, no bitcoin, no heritage. You just create the system and earn from it.

And again, what is richness? Who is rich? If you are not slave of the modern life, you are rich. I am not a millionaire. I just have some passive income, and that's all. I don't need to work anymore. I am only here to enjoy the life. This is the definition of being rich to me.

Good luck...

First, let me describe you the writing process. You must be imagining me, sitting in front of my computer whole day, typing, and deleting and writing... No, writing is not like that. You write while you walk, you write while you run, you even write while you sleep; but you write them in your head. Most of the writing happens when you are not sitting with a computer. You write into your head! While walking, eating, before sleep, after waking up, even while talking. These are the things that make the writing. And in the end, the actual writing just bursts itself onto paper in no more than thirty minutes!

Articles and research are different, you then need to sit and read and write with your very selective words that are not repeating itself and you need to give legit and proper source.

But for writing a book, as I said before, you think and write to your brain first and then you sit and give it all in one go.

And for this e-book subject, I can say this cover more than half percent of my passive income. I turned my hobby into an income, a dream came true, and it did not happen in one night.

It all started about 10 years ago when I wanted to write my memories into a word document and share them for my family. Then I thought, let me do a journal, then again, why not a book? This thought came into my mind, and I started writing my memories… I don't forget easily and because of that some friends call me elephant brain Burak or memory Burak.

I started writing my memories in a word document at work, at breaks, at journeys and at every possible location and time. They made about 400 pages! And I named it: "The Man who Lives in his Past" This became my first book, but it was in my native tongue, Turkish. Also, this book contained every memory of my childhood. I did not publish it first but found somewhere who can print them as a book and I just had about 10 copies for my family. They loved it and supported me. They always support me; family is the best.

After my first book, I wanted to write about my teenager years and I named it the same but added "2: University" I wrote all my university memories starting from year one until graduation, including summer holidays.

All went well and I submitted them to some well-known publishers to possibly have a printed book of mine. The process was so interesting and full of non-sense. You can only send your finished work to one publisher at a time which means you cannot send them to several publishers at the same time. Each takes three months to get a decision and you just sit and wait until you get a decline or an agreement. The biggest ones declined my work, they didn't find them worthy, or they didn't have the vision. This made me to try start-up publishers and some of them offered me to pay the cost of it. I didn't accept any of them, I didn't give up either…

I had such an original idea if I would have published it. I never told this idea to publishers, but I feel like I can share now as I don't see any reason why not. The idea was putting seeds into the cover of the book, yes, actual seeds. So, when people finished reading it, they would just bury the book and water it and what comes from tree would become a tree again. I don't know if anyone else has ever thought of that before, but this was also my idea if I had my book published as hard copy.

I started my third book, the fantasy one, meanwhile I started to think alternative ways to publish my books. Writing my fantasy book only took me a month because I love that subject. It was very easy and entertaining to me. I lived in the world that I created!

As soon as I finished my fantasy book, I went to the copier again and printed 40 copies to my family and best friends. Their feedback was important, and they really loved it. I wished I could have made it longer, or a series.

Getting likes for my fantasy book and having some free time made me write a poetry book and some very funny book that I couldn't even dare to print it. I really cannot remember the number of my Turkish books.

Thanks to my research, I found a way to publish them: E-Books! Why not? In the end, this was something completely free, and there was nothing to lose. I read about it, started minimising errors and thought about better cover designs.

I found a super easy and free way of cover designing which I will tell about it in another subject.

After getting them ready in PDF format, I created an account on Smashwords and started adding my works there. Smashwords is a dedicated site to e-books only. They have a service to provide free ISBN to any books. Otherwise, an ISBN costs 99 US dollars. I got my books assigned with ISBNs and standardised the formats of my books.

When you submit an e-book to Smashwords, it takes two or three days for them to publish it. Not only that, but they can also publish your book to many platforms including Apple Books. They do great work. All they get from this, is some cut after sales. Of course, they send you some tax documents to start your publishing and you say yes to every cut to make your work published.

The tax issue was okay at first but now it hurts when they cut hundreds of pounds each month, but this is the only fun fact. The other thing about Smashwords is they are not well known. The biggest e-book platform is Amazon. There is a handicap though, which is sadly Amazon does not accept Turkish books. I wrote them many times, but their reply was only saying that they are working on it. They are still working on it.

Back when I was in Turkey, I got a hit by government by banning PayPal in Turkey. This made my PayPal account useless, and cash got stacked up there. But I couldn't get the money from PayPal, so I let it stay this way. But when I moved to England in 2017, I connected it to my UK bank account, and I took my saved money from there which I earned by my hard work. It was enough to cover our one-year rent cost.

I am now about to tell you the big fish that I caught: Amazon! The first thing I did was, translating my fantasy book into English and changing the names in it and even changing the name of it to: "Blaad" And then putting it into Amazon Kindle Store. One of my greatest achievements in life. When people asked about me, I was only telling them to search my name on Amazon. Wow, this is not usual, is it? Now there are four books of mine on Amazon, and this will be the fifth.

Blaad gave me lots of courage and new ideas... I saw here that every book comes with characters, and they sell toys of it. At some bookstores, but usually the kids' section, I saw most of them have their teddies or plushies. I didn't want to pay for the merchandise, but this idea is staying with me for now...

Blaad was followed by a funny one which has a name of: "The Best 19 Bat Recipes for Hungry Tummies" and then followed by a very good one that I am very proud of: "F.A.Q. About Festive Cocktails & Mocktails" Both of them were written during pandemic and even though the first one is a complete fun way of cooking, the second one is a psychology book that focuses on inner self. Do not get confused by the cocktail or mocktail name, because it is nothing to do with recipes. Yes, I got some people disappointed by not finding cocktail recipes in it, but this was the breaking point of it. The last one of them was a child book which has the name of "My Bunny Rabbit: CottoBonto" and this one was only about 30 pages with big pictures in it. CottoBonto is the name of my last and only rabbit and I wanted to make his name and his story forever and gave it to my book.

I will also tell you about the cover designs of them and will share them but let me say this first that, all the designs were made by me, and it is unbelievably easy! And, free. You only need to use a Gmail account to sign into a webpage called Canva. I also used this page to create my NFT arts. Anyway, Canva is completely free and very user friendly and once you login, it asks you what you need to do and you choose ready to use designs from the list and you modify them. There is also a way to be a professional of this and design covers and logos and so and sell them, but this is not something that I have tried before. You can consider this option too if it looks right to you.

Designing Covers:

Now for my first design, Blaad, which was created by me using Canva in a few minutes only:

I only searched for vampire and found the vampire teeth and used some blurriness on it and socketed it behind the original cover. I changed the names and didn't add anything else and created this. As I said before, you don't need to be a graphic designer to do this, and you don't need to pay money. These examples that you see are completely free and can be done in minutes.

My second design for my other book, The Best 19 Bat Recipes for Hungry Tummies:

This design was used for a proper cookbook and again all I added was the bat icon on the top left. These images or items are royalty free by the way.

My best book that I am very proud of, F.A.Q. About Festive Cocktails & Mocktails:

This one took me some time because I created this from scratch and added only small images. I did the colouring of each letter by choosing the colours from the drinks and added Christmas effects to it. I also started the second book of this but still working on it. The name in my mind is F.A.Q. About Festive Cupcakes & Macarons. And we will see how it goes.

And last of all, my child book, My Bunny Rabbit: CottoBonto:

They all look very nice and simply, aren't they? As I said before, you don't need to be a professional to create an artwork like them, all you need is dedication and determination. Cover design should be under a completely new headline, I know, it is a very big subject when you choose this path but don't make a mistake by downloading an image from Google and neglecting the royalty of it, so just be careful about them and you will be fine.

There are also two optional covers that I designed for this book but chose the one that is on by having a vote with my family. I would like to show them here, to be honest, you would think I went too far on the last design, well, it was not my intention to do it but just for fun... Here they are:

This one with golden colours were my favourite however I was overvoted so I didn't use it.

But this one:

So, what would you think of the last one? I assume no one would buy it.

Your book does not need to be a best seller, and have you ever thought that, when you go to a bookstore, how come every book is a best seller? Especially or precisely, New York Times Best Seller? You must have seen this before and even guessed that. The answer is very simple, and it is like cheating, here it comes, if you can afford 10.000 copies of your own book or have enough friends or family to buy 10.000 copies, you can get it to the bestsellers list for a week, yes, that's a fact. And after that, you can technically claim that you are a bestseller author on your every future book that you are going to write, even if none of those books sell any copies, and even if your bestseller book never sells another copy ever again. This is a fact and maybe a glitch in the writing sector which I never tried and never needed to try though. Also, I heard another easy way that, to get on the best-selling list in some countries is easy, you just need to sell a certain number of books and to do this, you pay to a company, and they order, let's say 10.000 copies for themselves. Then you can ask the store or whatever place is selling your book that call the press and tell them that your book sold 10.000 copies in a day and boom, you are on the best sellers list.

Why am I telling you this? So that your encouragement does not go waste! There are lots of cheaters or bug exploiters in every part of the system and in every fragment of the life, do not forget that and never give up.

Articles: Writing articles and publishing them.

This subject is not so old for me, in fact it all started when I wanted to do a presentation to my teammates at work. It was about the future of artificial money. I did the presentation, sparked some discussion and I was asked to update about this subject in a few months' time… All was good but I wanted to do more, and I did more research on this subject and released an article on my LinkedIn account. It was a blast! Many friends and people that I did not know started messaging me and some even called me to congratulate and some of them started asking me questions about this subject, taking me as a professional.

I loved writing articles, getting likes and shares on LinkedIn was a first to me. I got invited for some speeches which I declined because I was not an expert but just a writer! The first article was only two pages by the way, including the sources and I will give it as an example soon.

After getting enough attention, which I don't like to be the centre of anything, I did not wait and started my next article. This time, I wrote something technical about Microsoft Excel and it was another blast! People wanted me to train them! Each article carried me to a higher place and gave me reputation.

I linked my articles with my YouTube Channel which you are about to read it on the next subject and by doing that, I added a link to my article, and I let the readers to listen the article with my voice... I also copied and pasted the full article into the description of the YouTube video.

Now you must be asking, how and when did you start earning about this? Well, it was a holiday time where I met an old friend and she advised me of some websites that takes articles and pays you. She also helped me to write another article where I got stuck. Thanks to her, I joined these websites and started to earn another passive income...

And what are these sites? As promised, I will give you full details of them. Firstly, LinkedIn does not pay you anything for the articles. It only helps you to advertise and get you known. They sometimes send surveys with rewards of £10 but it doesn't worth it.

Now there is one website, called medium.com, where you can create your own page and submit articles. After having more than 100 subscribers to your page, Medium starts to pay you, easy-peasy. You connect your LinkedIn and Twitter to Medium and start advertising your page. They keep you paying with one criteria, which is so easy, they only want you to write articles at least once every six months. The longer your article is, the more money you can make because this site has a program running behind that calculates the reading time of the viewers of your page.

Again, with great earning, comes great tax. But it is not that difficult to submit your tax forms that can be easily downloaded from the website and filled in a few minutes. They do the rest; they cut the tax and pay you the net amount.

Now back again to article writing and what did I do and how… I will show you some of my articles to make you see the pattern. They are all about future of a sector, or a field or anything that can have a future. So, every article of mine started with: "The Future of…" Not only that, each first paragraph started with: "Did you know…" Another pattern is the design of the cover of the article. Yes, there is a cover page. They all have same font type and same colours. So, if you want to be successful in article writing, you need to personalise it and create your own pattern.

And don't forget to include sources to them as it wouldn't be right if there were no sources. YouTube link is optional, it just gives another pattern to it, but I don't think it was the reason of success.

There is also a new trend that has been going on that I would like to mention about while in this subject, it is the Artificial Intelligence, where you can generate any article by using it, which I wouldn't recommend as it becomes so obvious you wouldn't expect great results by doing it.

Another point that should be here is, getting subscribers for your article page by buying subscribers. No, please don't go into this, the system understands this and also the system wants to see your link has been clicked every day, but these fake subscribers will only increase the traffic volume for a day and it won't do any good. Unless maybe if you can afford hundreds of thousands of subscribers, which I still have my doubts. So, just be yourself, and write your own articles.

My first written article was:

*Hi everyone, so I found this topic and I felt it would be
interesting and wanted to share with you. I hope you will
also find it interesting... And before I start, I want to say
that I am not an expert in crypto currency, and I will not
give any investment advise...*

*Did you know almost fifty percent of the world's central
banks are considering creating their own digital
currencies?*

*So, what is a Central Bank Digital Currency? It is basically
a digital money which is issued by a central bank, and it is
not based on any physical goods, making it completely
electronic. Their existence is like cryptocurrency, but there
are differences such as while a crypto coin can be issued
privately, CBDCs can only be issued by a central bank, and
they also promise that unlike crypto coins, the CBDCs will
not be risky, and instead they will keep their value and will
be reliable over time...*

*And what is the reason of creating Central Bank Digital
Currencies? The reason is simply creating better payment
services and improving the money. Same as other fields,
the way people use things and the way they choose to pay
is changing, and this new technology can be summarised
as adapting. And it is predicted that people will prefer
CBDCs over a bank account as CBDCs will not be at risk if
banks fail.*

And how will the Central Bank Digital Currencies work? It will have, as much in common with a bank deposit and will be as counterpart to a digital banknote. For example, people will deposit their cash, and they will be able to pay digitally, or transfer an account to make a payment. It is also important to say that if you convert a £20 note, it will always be worth same as the value that was converted which means there won't be any losses. Also, these currencies will not replace the current cash and bank deposits, but they will work alongside.

When will the CBDCs arrive? Some countries have already started implementing this; however, many countries are still in the development stage. The first country that introduced their CBDC was The Bahamas which happened in 2020. Nigeria followed this and became the first African country to establish their currency. India, Russia, and Sweden have started their trials and now they are testing their progresses. China is aiming to become the world's largest digital currency country and their goal is to start their currency to be used by the end of 2022. And in USA and in the UK, even though this has been signed and approved, it is still not yet decided to finalise it and the process is still under research status. So, in a summary, a total of nine countries have started using CBDCs and there are about 80 countries that are still in project conditions.

Will there be any benefits and any risks? The best benefit is the money laundering will be much easier to identify. Every transaction will be traceable. And there will be a better solution for some people, who cannot have a bank account, giving them the chance to have a CBDC account. Also, it is estimated that payment systems and financial *services will have potential for innovation and improvement...*

On the other hand, with great benefits, comes great risks... There will always be risks in cyber security and fraud. A security breach or an attack or a slight disruption will have an immediate effect on all payment systems and on consumers. So, it will be crucial to build the most secure and trustworthy platform otherwise CBDCs would not be successful without security that ensures user trust in the currency itself...

So, this is the summary of CBDCs. We will wait and see it together when they become online. I hope you found this interesting as well, and thank you for listening..."

I am not adding the source links or YouTube links to this one, but I hope this gave you enough sense to get the idea.

It is not that difficult to write an essay or an article when it is about one or two pages. All you need to do is getting the data by research.

Let me share you my second article so you can see the pattern easily:

"The Future of Excel: Power Query

Did you know you can use Power Query with zero knowledge of Virtual Basic or any other programming language?

So, what is Power Query and where do we use this? It is basically a data transformation tool with graphical user interface. This interface is so useful as it gives us the ability of interacting with set of menus and buttons. And the best part is, no knowledge of Virtual Basic is needed to use Power Query as it creates the coding by itself to do the transformation so we wouldn't be required to know any programming language which means mastering on Power Query is much easier... And where do we use Power Query? We use it for data analysis and business intelligence. In other words, Power Query makes the data more analysable.

The most common usage of Power Query is pivoting the data, and un-pivoting. Filtering data, creating custom columns, changing data types. And it can combine multiple tables, multiple tabs, and even multiple Excel files. So, analysts who like working with data started using Power Query to have quick and reliable results with unlimited options. And these can be used in any department, from finance to HR...

Where is the data coming from? It can be either one simple excel file or a simple PDF or a complicated SQL database or even web pages or cloud storages... You need to have a Microsoft Excel version above 2016 to be able to use Power Query as it will give you the option of "Get Data" menu.

A quick example? Let's say we have some financial data in a spreadsheet that has information of some products such as the country of origin of the products in a column and other columns have the order date, units sold, quantity, price and so on. When we load this data into Power Query, an editor will open. This editor generates the coding by itself as I said before so whenever we change something, a code appears in the background. We can go to this background to amend data manually but this requires some computing knowledge so we will leave it there. Anyway, this Power Query editor will give us some transforming tab where we can group some columns and sort them by region by units sold as an instance or price by country of origin. This is the most basic thing that can be done by Power Query: having a better, a helicopter view of the data.

If we go advanced, Power Query can be used to create real-time dashboards. This makes reporting much easier when it comes to present something to management. People use this to create financial KPI dashboards, sales cycle length dashboards, manufacturing production and procurement data analytics dashboards and human resources data dashboards. And if we go super advanced, Power Query can be used to create data models such as simple order management system or even an online shopping app or a hotel reservation system...

As I said before, the things you can do with Power Query is unlimited and you won't need to know any programming language to do that. All you need is clear data and what you want to do...

So, this is the end of this summary, I hope you also found it interesting and if I got enough attention and some demand, I would like to do an advanced session with real examples... "

This time, I shall tell you how I added the YouTube link so it can give you an idea if you intend to do it. So, I wrote exactly like this:

"Feeling tired? Why don't you watch and listen this article on Youtube:

https://youtu.be/0maV5dqs68s "

Let me add another point that could be put on the news feed of some users on LinkedIn. As soon as I finished an article, I quickly shared the link as a post on LinkedIn, gave the link of my article and the YouTube link and added hashtags on my post.

For instance, for my Excel Power Query article, I used these hashtags for the post:

"#excel #power #query #excelpowerquery #powerquery #digitalbanking #digitalassets #digital #future #datamanagement #data #dashboard #youtube #article #articleoftheday #articleoftheweek"

Now I believe these hashtags helped a lot. As you can see, some of them are general, some of them are specific hashtags.

Let me carry on with another article of mine that made me famous on some social media platforms among with bankers:

Did you know, it is not very far to move into a complete cashless society with some upgrades in banking?

So first, what are these upgrades going to be? Let's start with universal banking. Even though universal banking model was already established as a new feature, it is not yet being used in many countries and the model differs in every banking system. The most common usage of universal banking is, of course, being used in Switzerland along with some European countries. But what is universal banking? It is basically a variety of financial services that are connected to each other in the banking system including commercial, retail and investment services. And universal banks are basically commercial banks that offer a range of services, such as lending loans and accepting deposits under one roof, and the main advantage of this universal banking is merely being economically efficient in the form of lower cost, better output, and better products. And the qualifying notable banks that are considered as universal banks are Deutsche Bank, Bank of America, HSBC, and ING Bank, Wells Fargo, and JPMorgan Chase...

The second big step will be digitalisation in banking, which means a faster, more reliable, cost reduced, zero human error, gap eliminated system and more importantly a cashless transaction background. By going into this system, your funds and your records will be protected no matter what disaster or theft, or loss happens...

The digitalised system will lead a new FinTech era that is more focused on the fundamentals of "Know the

Customer" and will use data mining to gather signals via artificial intelligence and blockchain that can scan endless data, and as a result of this, new models of lending will be presented... And by legalising documents that are organised with blockchain will make the banks idle next to the FinTech companies in the future...

It is also important to know about the future of banking will work on satellite banking which is based on satellite telecommunication services that can be used as a backup in the event of natural disaster or a general failure where the connection is compromised.

And for the third one, as said in my previous article, CBDC (Central Bank Digital Currencies) will take charge of all but especially for people who currently rely on cash...

And with these three big upgrades in banking, in finance and generally in life, fraud and money laundering will have critical damage... These upgrades might also seem vulnerable to digital frauds such as cyber-attacks and data breaches, but these systems will cut the fraud in half...

Another major impact will be on the payment gateways... It is simple as every company will create their own payment system and, on account of that, companies will take their banking systems under their own... This is only the summary, but this massive upgrade will be told in my other article as it deserves more attention...

As seen above, if these systems merge perfectly, there will be huge improvement in the banking field that also covers the finance sector and payments system...

I saved the timeline of the promised cashless society in the end... As mentioned before, it is not that far, would you be surprised if I said this will happen very soon, maybe in a few years? Or maybe in 2026? Believe it or not, but this is the year that is foreseen by financial advisors..."

This article was only page, just a single page, the aftereffects, I mean the outcome was extraordinary. They invited me for some speech, I cannot believe it, just for one page of article... Not only that, but people also started asking me serious questions about their work.

Now I saved my biggest one for the last. I will share another article of mine, and this will be the last for this book. This time I completely wrote an article from my experiences and linked the source to myself. This wouldn't count as an article, but I couldn't find a section for this, and it ended up as an article.

Apparently, it was more than enough to arouse attention again that I got so many messages on LinkedIn and on other groups, and I gained too many followers on Medium.

Now let's see it:

"The Future of Recruitment: Crystal Clarity
Did you know the writer of this article, me, has gone through more than hundreds of interviews in about 20 years and if there had been an achievement of this, it would have appeared on my profile with a golden badge? Well, this is real, and because of that achievement, I found

myself worthy enough to share my experiences in this article. Take no offense but take them as improvement and motivation.

You may keep reading this article if you are not in top 1%, in other words if you are not holding the 45.8% of global wealth, in simple words if you are not in the rich category. Otherwise, you wouldn't be on LinkedIn or reading any articles but waking up on a yacht, and your only struggle would be deciding which port should you spend the day with your drink. But, if you are not coming from a family that holds a certain amount of wealth and doesn't need to work at all, this means you need to find a job for a living and you need to work until the time comes...

So, the journey begins...

Firstly, they call you and ask for some basic details such as work permits, location, the reason for willing to change your current role, notice period and check if you are suitable for this job and for the company, which is completely fine. The funny part in here is most of the recruiters are either newly graduate or have about six months of experience! And the company is asking for a senior level role or a manager for someone who has 20 years of experience in the field, and they are relying on a newbie recruiter to decide if this candidate suits this role or not... Some best matches cannot even pass this first stage because of the inexperienced recruiters and this false recruitment process. This first part does also make career changing impossible because of auto-elimination and they only look at your recent title. Everyone is after an easy life so if you started your career as a barista, they think you will be a barista until you get retired, because it is easy to them, and their system is created like that...

And secondly, please do take this seriously when advertising the job and please stop telling people that the holiday entitlement is one of the company's advantages. Holidays are not benefits! They are people's rights by law. If you want to talk about why the company is the best place to work, tell them about something that really is a bonus, maybe a day-off on your birthday, cycle to work scheme and gym subscriptions... Or just tell them how you approach on sick days and how you contribute to their pension... Tell them about how you dealt with the pandemic and what you did and how you treated your employees during the lockdown. Tell them about hybrid working and plans for future. You all ask us how we dealt with something when issues occurred or how we lead a project under difficult circumstances. You ask us so many questions like that but why don't you tell us about your side? These are the things that we want to hear, otherwise we all know that we all have 25 days of holidays wherever we go...

There is also another stage where we get asked about our qualifications. Since when certifications took over degrees? There are lots of us with master's degrees and even doctorate degrees, but when we do not have any certifications, we are identified as unqualified people. And telling the similarities of an MBA and ACCA or CIMA to a recruiter is a real pain... They just look at your certifications, don't care about your master thesis, your publications, or your six years of hard-earned Ph. D. and tell you that you are not qualified.

The journey continues...

Let's say somehow you were not eliminated by the automatic HR system or the programme that knows so much and eliminates candidates automatically by checking some keywords and you made it to the second stage where you are interviewed by two experienced people who are likely going to be your managers or supervisors. Here comes the routine questions such as tell us about a time, or give us an example of a time, etc... In here, you need to be the greatest faker if you want to get the job. It doesn't matter how super you are or how super you will be for the role. But you need to tell them some fantasy that never happened and give them what they would like to hear instead of facts to get the job.

It is mostly this second part of interview that decides if you get the job or not. I happened to get some questions that the answers should be entirely made up and cannot even get into the circumstances even if you intend to. When this mutually faking stage ends, some managers like to beat the candidates with their sector experience by asking them technical questions about the sector and the actual job... Once, I got a question by someone who asked me how to do double entry on a general ledger. My reply was only denying answering the question. Instead, I told them that these technical questions can be learnt by Google in two minutes; but if you hire me, you will work with me most of the day and I will be a part of your life, so maybe you should know more about me, you should learn who I am, what my personality is... You shouldn't question me with some non-sense technical questions where I can get the answers in a minute or two.

There is also another funny part in this second stage that when you are in a different sector and coming from another company, they take you for an alien or something like that. As for me, having several sector experiences, I always tell them that, you should break this thought and let other people contribute in diverse ways. They might be coming from another sector, but they might be thinking differently and by this variety of thought, things could be seen and challenged or even established in better ways...

The second stage usually ends after about an hour and if they tell you at the end that there will be other candidates too that they are going to interview, you should know that they didn't choose you. This is one of the keywords that one can experience and understand.

The journey goes on...

The last stage usually happens for formality, and this is the part where you meet with the director of the department whom you will never work with if it is a big company. They usually talk like they are in a rush and their only observation is focused on how you talk. This is because you might be presenting something to high management one day and they just want someone who can be able to express themselves. Confidence is the key in this final stage because there should be only you in this stage or maybe they are between two candidates, and you are one of them...

After the final stage, if they didn't call you for a very long time, and now they are suddenly calling you and saying that they accepted you; you should know that they hired the other person but then the other person left the role as soon as they get it, and now they are desperate and they need you as a last remedy. Also, it is quite possible that things go to the other way around and you might get an e-mail from the HR, saying they have feedback for you and want to speak with you. This feedback should be taken as a lesson and this is very valuable experience for you for the future interviews, do not waste this opportunity as most companies do not do that. This feedback is much better than receiving an auto e-mail with full of nicely selected words starting with "regret to inform" or "unfortunately".

The final stage could be otherwise too if you are lucky. The HR might suddenly call you just before sending the contract to tell you that you are hired and ready to be deeply checked and might give you the starting date. There could be some negotiations of salary during this call or not. They usually send you the contract afterwards and expect you to agree their terms... I can now tell you how you feel after getting this call; you are not sure if you did right or wrong, or if you are happy with that decision or not. Change is a risk and leaving your comfort zone is difficult, but it is necessary...

So, at the end, I better remind you that no offense should be taken as this article is only my experience and I hope everyone finds their dream job and every company finds their dream employee. And why crystal clarity? It is because everything is crystal clear, all you need to do is read the signs. If you are not the greatest faker, you need to focus and concentrate hard and work best to make a difference. This applies to the interviews and to the work. Good luck!

#recruitment #humanresources #crystalclarity #future #finance #youtube #article #articleoftheday #articleoftheweek #articleofthemonth

Feeling tired? Why don't you watch and listen this article on Youtube:

https://youtu.be/Hy-ZnnJ7gy0

Sources:

Me "

This time I added the full article to show you the big picture. Now let me add the cover image that I talked about. As I said before, all covers have the same style, font type and colour:

The Future of Recruitment:

CRYSTAL CLARITY

BY BURAK CINAR

So, before I share the last article, I should say that if you are trying to get subscribers, you should be writing in general subjects. If you write something that is very specified, you can get recognition. That is why I am sharing this very specific subject that this article has got. And the name of it is: "The Future of Accounts Payable: Resolutions"

"The Future of Accounts Payable: Resolutions

Did you know that automating the Accounts Payable is not going to be what it was thought to be?

There is a trend for each sector and each job type that comes with automation and Artificial Intelligence, well, this is still not going to happen in Accounts Payable for a long time and if you are actually into these fields, you will see what I mean. While technically, some of the automation would work on certain areas of Accounts Payable, not every aspect can be fit into the criteria of Artificial Intelligence therefore it leaves a big area for resolutions.

In other words, if we divide Accounts Payable into three sections, such as postings, resolutions and payments, there is no such software or system that can do the resolutions part. The only part that can be done automatically is the payments side, apart from the approvals. The posting of invoices can also be done automatically but limited. There are still some countries that rely on paper, and you must know that each type of invoice is different; however, these are not the only factors. The importance of Accounts Payable will always be essential in order to keep strong relationships with the supplier. What happens if you don't pay an invoice? You won't get the service or the goods, it is that simple. While Accounts Payable is very underrated, it reflects the company's face which needs to shine.

What comes under resolution then? Resolutions starts with supplier master data, such as creating and setting up a vendor to do payments and for this, there must be a human who does the actual controls with a supplier and a bank by phoning them and talking to them. Some companies put this role under other accounting departments for being coherent with segregation of duties or delegation of authorities, but this still applies to Accounts Payable. The works of resolution continues with queried or parked invoices which takes the most valued parts of resolutions. Then adding statement reconciliations with vendors would be smart to be at the same page with the supplier and spot any missing invoices to prevent disruptions.

There will always be ad-hoc works under resolutions such as in GRIR (American version) or GRNI (European version) to find out goods or works that need to be invoiced or the cause of not yet being invoiced. Debit balances that can be another point of view where it can get messier without someone looking after it and managing properly. On the other hand, the aged items that haven't been resolved after a year or so, will also be inevitable and will needs lots of manual work to resolve them. Controlling expenses of the employees or payrolls would also be described under resolutions but this mostly does not and should not *fall on the shoulders of resolution side of the Accounts Payable.*

Let's say the posting and payment side of Accounts Payable were completely automated, yet there will be manual payments such as pre-payments or down-payments but okay let's say these sections were automated, this would still leave a big work for the resolutions side. There needs to be a human to look after the queried invoices. A human need to chase the procurement department, the supply chain department, or any relevant department for receipting or in other words GRNing services, works, deliveries or parts, items, and goods. Another manual work is also needed for the discrepancies, such as inconsistent prices or irregular quantities, where the automation cannot do anything. The resolutions person or the team need to be there to contact with people on the queries and resolve them.

Another point to mention is compliance and in terms of that, each company needs to adapt the latest governance by following updates. American companies for example need to comply to SOX requirements and to do that, in a very basic instance, each transaction must contain an attachment that holds a proof of the nature of the transaction.

How would the automation work then? It can still work - even for now- with small companies that doesn't have a workload of paying invoices and those that holds only a certain type of invoices. Designing an automation for small companies is quite easy and it works fine. They did not need an Accounts Payable department in the first place! But for very large companies where the department holds more than 20 people, there hasn't been an automation system created yet and it doesn't seem to do it in the near future. Yes, there are systems that can recognise a purchase order number and differentiate it with the invoice number but not in every scenario. And yes, there are tools to validate data and approve invoices by amounts, but they are simply not enough. They mostly fail when multi-currencies and multi-taxes are getting involved.

Some companies also prefer humans over automated systems as sometimes the costs of implementation and the costs of sustainability become similar; but this is another point of view. The variety of tools and software are too many to consider and when it comes to decide, companies usually go old school.

For the conclusion, there are so many areas that still need to be done manually in Accounts Payable and there is no such Artificial Intelligence yet to cover the areas of resolutions; and, if anyone says that Accounts Payable has no future and all will be automated, you can tell that they know nothing of Accounts Payable... They can change the name of the Accounts Payable and they can tell that they have automated everything; but no, there will always be people that does the extra work of resolutions and the importance of Accounts Payable will remain..."

As you can see, the last article is only appealing for a very specific and a limited area. The choice is yours, and let me say, by being an expert in Accounts Payable, this article above took me only half a day to write. On the other hand, I also wrote another article about the future of accountancy, but it got me only a few likes. Again, it is not easy to get the right timing and right hashtags...

I hope these were helpful and if you choose to become an article writer to make some money, I will be gladly sharing more information if you get stuck at some point.

Just don't forget to add sources, hashtags and be yourself. Create your own pattern and style it to represent your ideas. Always trust yourself and stand up for each word.

The top article writer on Medium is earning 49K according to Google and any average writer like me can earn about 1K which is more than enough by doing nothing but writing some articles time to time. This is a good money, as again, being rich is not about being a millionaire, it is about earning by the systems that you created. This way of earning is really the easiest of all. If you enjoy writing and have time to do it each week or month, follow this path as you won't regret.

Big ones for passive incomes:
YouTube: Creating a channel, uploading and monetization.

Now this one is a very funny one. No matter how hard I tried, I still couldn't figure it out the pattern of getting views and likes. You will see what I mean when I show you but believe me, if you get to be a partner of YouTube with your channel, you will never need to work again.

YouTube just asks you for at least 1000 subscribers and 4000 hours of watching time per month. When you ensure these prerequisites, you will get an email from YouTube about being their partner. Or you can try the channel monetization link from your YouTube studio menus. It will show you the progress of where you are right now.

Creating a channel is easy, all you need is a Gmail account. You login to YouTube with your account and you just click the create a channel link from settings or the menu above. Then you get an area where you can customise your channel with access to YouTube Studio. These are the things that you can explore easily if you are interested in this path.

So, about the views, which I mentioned that I couldn't figure it out what's the reason behind. There I will show you two of my short videos. First one is just 7 seconds, and an elf toy is sliding on a slide in a playground, that's it, no effects, no music, nothing. Just a toy on a slide, and it got 129K views! Also, it has 1.6K likes! I really do not understand it.

Check out this one with 129K views:

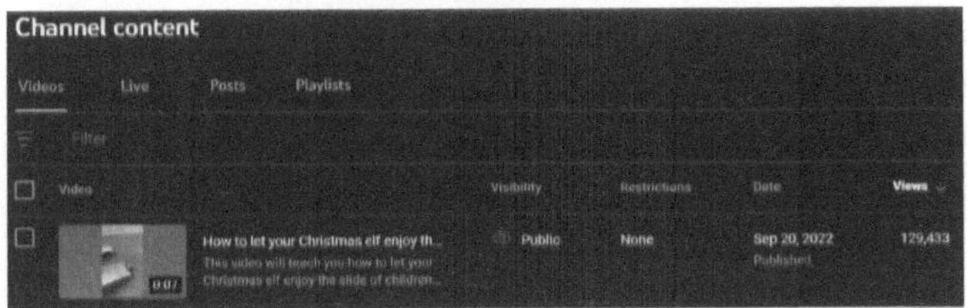

The second video is me stroking a dog while sitting next to river. It has nothing special about it and it is only 12 seconds. They both have the same hashtags if you ask about it but this one got only 27 views. Why? Is it all about luck or timing? This is the thing I couldn't figure out.

And see this one with 27 views:

Anyway, the secret of being successful is making short videos to get subscribers. There is a big handicap here, the watching time doesn't count on short videos so use this for getting only followers. There is only a special thing about shorts which was recently introduced and still at testing phase, they ask you to have 10 million watches for your shorts in the last 90 days. Not too bad for a shorts streamer but it is a pain for beginners.

Just do what I did, take a 10 second video of an animal, a grass, a toy, or anything. I always used a pattern again in all videos and they all start with "How to..." So, the style of the successful channel was only fun. Another tip here for short streamers, again no reason why but if you upload a short video which is over 15 seconds, it doesn't get featured and you get very less views. So, keep them below 15 seconds to make them available for all.

Here are some headlines of my short video uploads to give you some heads up:

"How to spot a spaceship in woods and wait for aliens and get scared and excited step by step..."

"How to view a Halloween Garden House and enjoy pumpkins with witch, and decorations step by step..."

"How to pet your cutest cockapoo poodle dog and love it with care and joy step by step...

"How to get in love with autumn nature and leaves and hum lovely, cute Snowman song step by step..."

"How to observe an Ent from Lotr and hum Silent Night Christmas Carol on bridge walk step by step..."

"How to open horadric altar and get dupe on Diablo Immortal and close it immediately step by step..."

"How to watch dogs and swans and geese playing and getting along together in forest step by step..."

"How to spot a pirate ghost ship on River Thames and zoom in for Halloween step by step..."

"How to complete London Underground metro map puzzle 1000 pieces and proudly show it step by step…"

"How to squeeze an orange sensory fidget squishy toy and play with it step by step…"

"How to walk on muddy puddle for Peppa Pig as an adult and enjoy mud pool step by step…"

"How to get ready for quality Fish and Chips with vinegar and salt and peanut oil step by step…"

"How to get ready for pandemic lockdown by stacking up crisps and beers step by step…"

"How to mine and collect shiny mineral rocks as Amethyst, Ruby, Sapphire, Emerald step by step…"

"How to feed and entertain your bunny rabbit by letting him eat the fresh veggies step by step…"

"How to ready sizzling pepperoni salami on induction oven and prepare good breakfast step by step…"

"How to play with blue blob fish huge, big balloon step by step…"

"How to play with battle bugs and pet beetles step by step…"

"How to play with cute scary horrorful squishy Goujitsu and squeeze slimy skins step by step…"

"How to explore a sunken ghost ship in River Thames and think of huge Titanic step by step…"

Now I believe these were enough to give you the tips of the style.

I found out that some keywords and timing apply to viewing or it is just my imagination. For example, if I put the words or hashtags something like banana, food, Christmas, elf, the video gets more hits. But if I put some words like duck, swan, nature, jungle, the video doesn't get enough attention. This might be a fact or not, still trying to figure out. And found out that, if you mark your videos "made for children", they cannot be commented on and they get less views. This could be a fact or not though.

Here is an example of it:

As seen above from the screenshot that the nature video got only 13 views while others have gone over 1K. The popcorn video got 12K for no reason. I uploaded the elves videos at the same time and with the exact same words and hashtags but one of them got 3K and the other one got 1K views. Maybe I should come up with a conclusion that these are all random and all about luck.

Anyways, getting subscribers to your channel is the key and uploading easy and funny short videos to your channel is the solution to it. Once it hits above 1K subscribers, you can focus on long videos that can get you watch time.

There are too many pages and groups in Facebook for people who want subscribers or watching times. Some groups have 300K members. But they never work! When I first created a channel, I advertised it maybe 100 times on these groups and none of them joined my channel. Some of them messaged me, asked sub4sub, which is a term for subscribe my channel so I will subscribe yours, I agreed but after subscribing my channel, they left a few days later. Seriously, 300K members have the capacity to make each other rich on YouTube, they have nothing to lose, but they are all haters that only they want to be rich, and they never support each other, full of haters. So, never ever spend your precious one second there, on these worthless Facebook groups. Don't rely on anyone, rely on your videos.

YouTube also becomes very addictive once you start getting paid by them. You will also get messages or email from some product owners that they want you to advertise them and in return they offer free products and even some cash. This only starts when your channel becomes famous.

It is good to mention that when you become a partner of YouTube, you become a premium member. No more ads, and no more disturbance while watching or listening something.

And about the watching times, the thing I did was the most successful of all other videos that I published. I found an eight-hour non-stop royalty free Christmas music, non-stop, complete 8 hours! I edited the cover, but it took some time to upload it to the video editor and again uploading into YouTube, but it paid off.

If you are a very first starter of a YouTube channel, you can consider creating some Gmail accounts by yourself, maybe about 3 or 5 just to subscribe your channel and if you have a very long video, you can change IP and watch them from your accounts to get a kickstart.

Shall I tell you how many channels I have had over years? About five... All four of them were a failure. Only the last one shined and made my second biggest income. So, what were the four of them? A horse masked man doing some funny stuff, a guy reading books to children in a very funny way, a red violin guy playing his violin with Christmas songs at the background and another one that tells fun facts about stuff. All of them couldn't even made above 100 subscribers and they all failed. Again, I did not give up. I read about some pages and forums and created my last channel. I am glad I did that.

Another funny stuff that should be here is, I happened to find out some programmers are just writing a code on Python that finds and downloads the royalty free videos or music from the internet, then cuts and makes it a new video, and uploads to the channel in every six hours. Automation, even for that! However, after seeing the examples of how rubbish videos they could be, I can say, nobody would ever watch them! But still a good idea, if I hadn't seen this example, I would have never guessed or would have never thought about the possibility of that code.

Believe me, this way of getting rich is both easy and free and fun! And if you can turn this into a very professional way, you won't need to do anything else for the rest of your life.

As you all know or as you have all done this before, I will not start by telling you about how to create an account as this technical knowledge is not the purpose of this book and it would be time wasting. The key point in here is, you should not lose faith when you see other similar groups or accounts. You know, most of the people lose it before they start in any job. They say that this was done by someone else, no, you shouldn't think like that. Very basically, think of a computer game on a mobile phone, there are maybe hundreds of the very similar game and still every one of them has millions of downloads. So, if you are willing to create a group for books as an instance, you should still create it with a simple name like "Book Readers and Writers". Yes, there are hundreds of them, but they are still working fine. Same as Instagram, take a bunny account like mine as an instance, there are maybe thousands of them, and still working fine.

I created an e-book Facebook group and an Instagram account for my bunny, CottoBonto. I created them after learning from my mistakes. I had another Instagram account with more than 1000 posts. The follower number couldn't even reach to 3000 and likes were about 10 or 20 for each post. It was because I only used hashtags when posting something. I understood that, sometimes you need to write some information, use correct and original hashtags, and need to tag some people or business accounts to be successful. My idea for my bunny Instagram account was giving facts about rabbits.

In order to grow on Instagram, I started with quality posts over quantity and searched for most searched hashtags. I studied on rabbits and under each post, I wrote a fact about rabbits' life or breeding them or any useful information of bunnies as a pet. I found some very famous bunny accounts and tagged them on my post and commented about something by tagging them. Then I saw some posts are getting more attention when they are posted by using videos or reels instead of plain pictures. I started recording my bunnies' videos and posted them as reels. As mentioned before, you need to go for quality over quantity. This is the key element and it worked perfect.

Another point of view of mine was creating memories for my son, so I created this Instagram account for my son and turned it into a small business. It doesn't need to be a business account though; your account will get known after having 10K of followers. Then it will allow you to share links of stories and you will be eligible for monetization, same as YouTube.

All this applies to the Facebook group, as it also needs quality but in here, you need to manage your group on an hourly basis, or you can hire volunteer admins for your group if you trust them. You need to welcome every member and create original posts to keep your group growing. After having more than a thousand members, the group will enlarge by itself.

There is another funny stuff about them when getting known. Some companies will start messaging you, asking you to advertise their product on a second page of your post. For example, for my bunny account, I was approached by a backpack company and was offered three different backpacks and was asked to advertise them. My first instinct was, comparing bunnies with backpacks and thinking of a scam. But no, they were legit, I just needed to take my rabbit's picture next to the backpack. It followed with breweries and were offered lots of free beers and wines and sherries! It became a very fun way of getting freebies. Not only earning money, but I also got the chance to try not well-known brands.

It is also essential that I should also tell you that, some of the freebies are not free. They charge for postal fee which doesn't seem ethical because some of the items that I was offered were free, that was okay but the fee for postage and packing were ridiculous. It is of course up to you when making the decision but go for the complete freebies. I was even offered to do a post with a shaver with my bunny, no idea how the advertisement became successful, but it was free anyway…

The main idea of this is getting paid by ads, and by getting into this level, you really need to spend some time on your page to get known. Don't forget that you should always work on quality over quantity and don't do the mistake by buying followers or subscribers to your page or group. It can be spotted easily and can have a negative impact on your real followers. Do not invite people to your group constantly either, only one would be enough, and if you give really good information or provide something useful, it can be shared by other people and one day you can reach your target. You should learn the way of using creative content and another way of getting your job done by other people. To do this, all you need to give them something that doesn't get forgotten easily. Then people will do the rest, they will share, share, and share and your page or group will evolve.

Your page or group doesn't need to be unique, don't forget that there are several pages that are exactly the same, but they all have 300K followers. Don't let yourself think that you need to do something very original that no one has done it before, no, this thought is wrong and can make you unsuccessful and this is the way of some jealous people that want you to lose. They will tell you that there are tons of same groups, or ideas, or anything like that. Do not listen to them, do you know how many successful pages or groups like that? They share the exact same content and idea, but they are all getting what they want to get. Another example, do you know, how many games that have completely the same logic, but they are still having millions of downloads? So, do not fall into that trap and freely create the exact same group. People like to join stuff like that, and they really want to continue their old habits, because they don't like change, but they can try something very similar to what is in their comfort zone. Before each innovation, successful or not, you should have some empathy and think about what you would do or how you would think. There is no need to rush when creating the system, instead, every step needs to be measured carefully...

Even though growing pages or groups and getting paid by the ads and enjoying freebies was the main idea of this topic, there is another way of getting some money in this. Once you learnt to build a successful page, you can create another and sell the previous one. A group that has 50K followers in it costs about 500 pounds and so. There are some platforms that do the exchange, but I haven't tried this way as I have no intention of selling any of my accounts. It should be simple as selling a game account so googling this will give you some solutions if you want to have some quick money by selling them, it is your way of getting rich, so it is your decision. You can also have some boost up and buy a group like that but only if you think you have enough time to grow it up.

Big ones for passive incomes:
Spotify: Creating your own music, distributing your album, and earning royalties.

This one comes with natural ability and some performance but after doing it, you will get royalties until your life or agreement ends. Before I start, I should say that this is still in progress on my to-do list and haven't started it yet. I did lots of research though and I will share my knowledge with you.

The beta version of upload your music to Spotify started a few years ago but it was with invitation only, and now it is not that difficult to do this. You get paid when your fans or anyone stream your music on Spotify, it is that simple. The funny part is, Spotify doesn't charge you any fees or commissions no matter how frequently you release your music. There will only be charges if you work with a distributor though.

There is a complete artists guide on Spotify webpage so I would recommend reading it first but let me encourage you by saying that the process is easy to start. People usually records themselves and uploads their performance on their YouTube page and wait for distributers to find them. This is also okay but why wait when you can do it by yourself? Just download the app "Smule" for free and start doing your own songs or sing karaoke on royalty free music. If you have some budget, you can find a studio and create your music and sing your song professionally.

Create your own album cover by using the free platform Canva again and think of a funny nickname. Take your own picture and play with it, make it look unique or very charismatic. You don't need to advertise your album, all will be done by other people, they will like it and add it into their lists, and they will share. Once they share, you will be successful in this.

Let me mention that, if you google selling your own music or adding your own music to Spotify, you will see lots of webpages that attracts you to them, you can try them but think of them as contributors so get ready for paying commissions to them if you agree to work with them.

I shall also add my opinion on being a basic or a premium member of Spotify, well, I have both. To be honest, I like listening to ads sometimes, it is good to have something to disturb you time to time, especially during pandemic, I learnt that someone called Peter did millions of shuffling on Spotify for no reason and lots of useful broadcasts by government. The ads and skipping music get painful so when I want to explore some music without disruption, I take my other phone which has the premium version of Spotify and I start listening from there. Believe me, I enjoy more on my basic account, that's why I am keeping it for my primary account for statistics... And yes, even though nobody cares, I love keeping my listening statistics on Spotify, as it reflects my soul...

No one finds you by chance and no one begs you to do something, it is all you that must do something, so if you think you have the ability for singing, go for it. Good luck!

Big ones for passive incomes:

NFT: Creating a wallet, designing NFTs, and selling them on market.

There is a special part on my YouTube account that tells everything about wallets and NFTs and I have videos of them telling you how to start your own work step by step. On that particular video, I created a wallet on Metamask, I created an NFT from scratch and I created a market on a free website and put it online. This whole process took about 30 minutes.

All you need to do is, taking a picture of something and converting it into an NFT. Rest it easy and technical, you can either watch that video or of course there are several of them or you can simply learn it by googling it.

To be honest, I was late when I learnt about NFTs, and this train was gone. I created many markets and many NFTs but couldn't get what I wanted. All my earnings from NFTs went into my Ethereum wallet and turned into cash but if I had done that one year ago, I would have been a millionaire. Well, being a millionaire was never my target or was never my intention, but there is serious money in this business if you are willing to. Let me remind you again that, being a millionaire will not make you happy.

As your guide, firstly you need a wallet and all you need to do is googling Metamask. Creating a wallet is like creating an e-mail account. Only difference is, instead of a password, you will get a combination of words.

Then, you need a free website that doesn't charge you for putting your items on the market. They call this gas fee, and this is hurting when your NFT is about 100K because they charge you before you sell them which is a great risk. To prevent this, I found a website called, Mintable, and by using it, the website charges you only after you sell it.

Third part will be taking a picture of anything. My successful sales were from my bunny pictures and my gonk pictures. Very simple, take one nice picture and convert it into an NFT format using a website called Fotor. Again, completely free. I mentioned Canva in the part where I talked about book covers, this one also works, your choice.

Let me show you some examples of my NFTs...

My NFT Designs:

This is my bunny, CottoBonto, right after having a shower and there is a small scarf on its head. This is it, Fotor turned it into an NFT, and guess how much I got by selling it? 10K GBP! Yes, I put it on the market for 10K and someone bought it! I wonder what they did with this picture afterwards... I heard that some filthy rich have too much money, almost endless, and they just want to spend it to anything they see. Anyway, the Mintable website cut their fee and after a week later, it went into my wallet, and it was about 9.5K.

Another one:

If I knew, I would put this on market for more, because I
was only trying this website and all I got from this picture
was 1K GBP... Still not bad, the net amount that I got was
950 GBP but after seeing this, I created about hundreds of
NFTs and created some marketplaces. I didn't use a single
marketplace but created a few of them, in case, they get
stolen or banned for some reason.

You can also draw something on paper and take its
picture and convert it into an NFT but why would you

need that? Just take a simple picture by your phone. It is unbelievably easy!

Sadly, at the first of 2022, Elon crushed the market of NFTs and coins, so my earnings from NFTs have decreased harshly and I stopped working on them. Yes, there are still marketplaces of mine, but they don't sell a lot, because people do not buy them a lot.

If you are really into it, I would recommend that please watch and learn how to create it and publish it, learn about it, then start doing it. Otherwise, you might end up with paying gas fees for nothing, be careful about this. Start with small amounts or maybe free images, and create your own brand in the market, get well known, then play big. There is no losing and risk free when you start gasless platforms so take it as an experience and use it.

Good luck!

The Only one with some budget:

Airbnb Business: Partnering or owning an Airbnb business that can cover its expenses and gives you back in time.

This is the only one that might need a budget but there is also a free way to do this as well. I know I said that every path will have zero cost but if you are willing to spend about 10K, this business will grant you £500 - £800 each month with zero effort.

Let's start by telling you this. There are some people whose only work is running Airbnb business, renting houses or flats in big cities, and assigning cleaners and advertising them on their Airbnb business accounts. The only thing they do is getting some items in the flat or the house and advertising it. The system that they create does the rest. They can manage everything and invest all by themselves or they sometimes need a partner if they are a start-up.

What I did was, I partnered up with someone that had a few flats in London, and I signed a contract with him on a suit for a year. I just wanted to try this first to see if it really something or a scam. And this is how it works. The rent of the suit was 3.5K each month, the cleaner and Airbnb fee were not that much but it was still something. But renting a suit does comes with a lot of details, you need to pay for deposit and two rents in advance and you need to buy the items for the flat. Thanks to the guy who was my partner, he did all that, but the contract was holding both of our names. Everything including double rent costed me 10K and another 10K to him.

The agreement with you and the partner can be done by half-half or you can change it by depending how much you invest at the beginning. We decided to pay 50-50 so we got the net profit by half.

It really went well; I haven't even seen the flat. All I did was, paying the 10K and getting the profit each month. The partner used to send me details of who rented it, who cancelled it, who did this and that...

Thankfully the contract was ending just before the pandemic so when we saw what is coming next, we cancelled everything and ended the contract just before the lockdowns. If we didn't do that, I think we would lose all the profit by paying rent for a flat that doesn't have customers at all...

After the pandemic ended, I reached my partner again and we started this business again. He has now more than 20 flats on Airbnb, and he hired someone just to manage the bookings and responding the customers. I am partnered with him again on several flats and my earnings from there exceeds 5K each month. All have profits and zero headaches. If I happen to have a single issue with any of them, I have the luxury to cancel my contracts because I am no slave and I am free...

At the beginning, I also told you about a completely free way of Airbnb investing. While I don't recommend it, this is still something that one can think about if they are willing to take some risks. The partnership also offers a way that the zero-money investor gets all the risk and gets their name on the contract only and get 20% of profit each month. Only do this if you can afford losing some money but it may be the other way around, depending on your partner.

Some people think they can do this all alone but trust me, it comes with lots of stuff, such as taking the keys, cleaning, minor repairs, and all like that. It can't be a single person job. If you want to take this risky path, do your research, and choose your partner carefully... Again, good luck!

There is big fish here if you have some time to spend and if you like socialising. Best way to start is having a LinkedIn account so that you can connect and contact with people. There are several websites that works only on referrals. There are also recruitment agencies that can pay you referral fees if your candidate is successful. You can simply google, refer a friend to job, and find these agencies. But they don't pay well, they only pay you around £150 or £300, depending on the role and to do this, they want the candidate to be a permanent employee and to complete their probation period.

As for me, I wanted to catch the big fish and found a website called Referment, they also have an app now. They used to pay a lot when they first started, such as 3K or 4K, and it was not only for permanent roles but also contracts. They even used to give you £50 Amazon vouchers if they only made it to the interview stage. Now they reduced their prices, but it is still worth to try it.

Now if I check my account, I see that I referred over 100 candidates to certain jobs. Half of them made it to the interview and ten percent of them got the actual job. I earned a lot from this. And I only worked during my train journeys while I used to do 20 minutes of train journeys each day while working at a nice family company.

I read the job description of the role that I was going to refer first. Then went into LinkedIn and searched for people whose headlines were mostly about open for opportunities and with their expertise. I sent messages to them and asked if they would like to be reached for this role. I only sent them the screenshot of the job descriptions and if they agreed, I would pass their details to the referral site. I must have contacted about a thousand people and only twenty percent of them were interested in. Most of them thought that I was the recruiter, but I told them that I am only referring them.

This was all I had to do! Look easy, isn't it? Well, it was very easy. You don't need to speak with them, just get their permission to pass their details to the referral agency and that's it, let them do the job. Then you get notified by e-mail that your candidate made it to interview stage and they got the job and stuff like that. I turned my train journeys into a money-making efficient way, and I was proud of it. Now I don't need to do this because I don't need it.

If you have large connections and if you have time to do this, I can tell you that this is a very easy money. The only thing you should be careful about is passing their details and getting their permission. Never submit someone's CV or any details without letting them know.

Another good thing about this referral is, if the candidate gets another job because of you in one year, you get awarded again. They keep the candidates' details for a year and even if they find them another job, you get your reward anyway because in the end it was you who submitted their CV to them.

Now I would also like to tell you about an experience of mine which made me almost give up, but I didn't. Firstly, about five years ago, I saw someone writing something on a wall, it was: "They want you to give up!" and then he wrote: "Never give up!" These writings on the wall were also carved into my brain. They became my motto. Each time I saw someone trying to make me give up, I always think of that... There will be haters always, and they will try to stop you for being successful, they want you to stay as you are or even worse so they can be happy. And their happiness is coming from your sadness. I have had enough of these people. Thanks to the man who was painting those wise words to the wall, I did not give up!

And yes, for the experience, which was not a good one to remember, I found someone on LinkedIn for a certain job and kindly sent her an invite, sent the job description, and asked her if she is interested. Her response was terrible, she wrote a lot of things that nobody would want to hear, took me to a conman, or an identity thief. My reply was nothing, all I did was blocking her. But the negative affect on me for some time remained. Because of my non forgetful mind, I live things that I experienced in my mind continuously and I think of every possible detail. It only made me sad, again as I said, I was about to give up on this, but I didn't. I wouldn't let a ruined one to ruin my dreams... So, be the same, remember that haters want you to give up, do not let them...

Keep referring people to correct jobs and this can be your only job. Just keep track of your referrals and be approachable and be honest. This is the real deal...

There are other small ways of referrals too, but they wouldn't worth it. For example, if you are using Vodafone, you can refer a friend for the same company through your account and you can get £50 vouchers easily. It is just about googling and about how you want to spend your free time.

Small Bits:

Game Accounts: Creating, building, and selling game accounts.

This one comes with joy if you like playing online games. The game needs to be online otherwise there are no possible ways to sell your account. I only tried it twice and both worked, however you need to enjoy the game first, otherwise this would turn into a torment.

You should find a very popular game and if it's possible you should be one of the first ones to try these games.

There is a new online game called Diablo Immortal and because of my interest to this game, I was one of the early access gainers. I played the game for a month, enjoyed every little bit then wanted to sell the account. Again, the key point in here is, selling a game account must be done when there are not too many players around the world and when they are all hungry for power. I recently found a Diablo Immortal game account for $250 to show you and here how it looks:

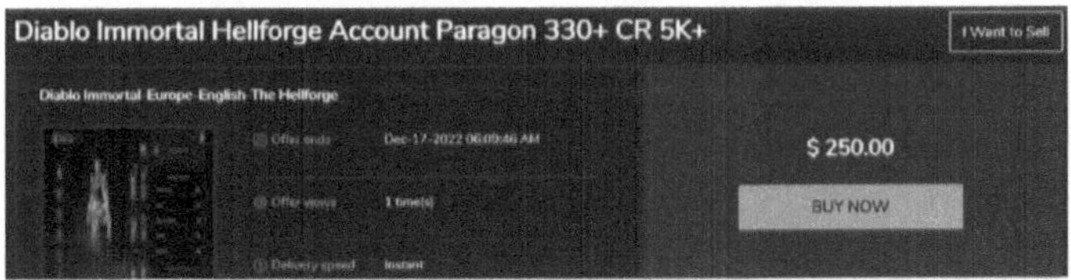

Another one I just got to show you for another online game:

Now that you got the point, let me tell you where to publish your accounts.

The one I used and tested is playerauctions.com and another one is g2g.com

You don't need to submit any of your detail to list in player auctions but g2g needs your ID so you should know this in advance. If you are selling more than three accounts in a month, you need to add them into tax assessments by filling the tax forms in there easily. Getting paid is also done by several methods but there is always a cash payment option into your bank account as well as Skrill or PayPal. Skrill is also a platform where you can convert your cash into coins.

This way of earning is considered a very cheap way of earning but if you enjoy games, don't let your accounts go waste and sell them easily, that's what I would do.

Game Items: Selling game items on online games.

Another way to have some pocket money, again if you are willing to spend some time on gaming. Let me tell you that there is a big market for only online game items. You wouldn't believe if I told you that I sold a colourful sword in an online game for around 2K US dollars to a guy a few years ago. Well, the drop rate of this sword was 1/300 and the chance you can get it was once a month so it was super rare, but can you believe it, a random guy or maybe a kid is paying 2K US dollars for an item in a game.

And now people buy and sell game items for Bitcoin or just doing the transactions over crypto; but I still believe that easiest is using the web pages which I just told you on the game accounts part.

If you are into a business that works on getting commissions on transactions, you should bear this in mind that this is the real deal. Thousands of transactions are being made on these websites and the commissions are about five percent and imagine the outcome just after a single day.

Let me show you a screenshot of an item for a popular game which is called CS: GO

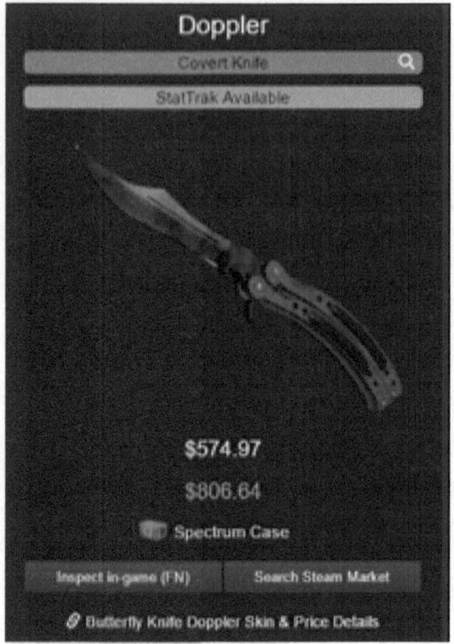

The reason of the high cost is only its rare colour. That's it! People really like cosmetics and appearance that make no difference in game which I never understood.

So, if you are a real gamer, consider these two ways of getting some pocket money, easy-peasy!

Much More Small Bits:

Parking: Renting your garage or driveway.

This one seems funny if you are not living in England or Europe, but it is a very common way to rent your garage or your driveway to people in here. Again, there are some websites or apps to advertise it and I chose "JustPark" app to do this.

It is so simple, all you need to do is to provide pictures, address, and good information. My driveway has capacity to hold two cars and I have a garage too but didn't offer our garage for some security reasons.

To be honest, one time a stranger wanted to rent my garage for a week for a very expensive brand car and I thought what if it is stolen and trying to hide it and what if I got into trouble. Then I said to myself that, no headache but easy work, so just the driveway.

I now have a Ring camera that captures the movements within my driveway, and I don't see any handicaps or issues with this.

People find my ad on the app, and they book slots easily. I get notification by e-mail and SMS and the good thing is we don't even need to speak or see each other. This is now a thing now; people do not want to talk to each other. So, they come and park and leave. They do the payments on app, and I got paid after the cut. There is only one thing that you need to be careful about, just do not let them clash by having several apps, otherwise it becomes a pain when two cars book your place at the same time.

You can amend the costs on the app easily and you can see other driveways that can be an example when determining the cost. I usually become the lowest as possible to be helpful.

What I earn, gets on my PayPal account and I spend them on pubs, so basically, I drink the money. Good luck...

Another Bunch of Small Bits:

Software Reviews: Writing honest reviews on software that you use.

Do this only if you need quick cash but be careful, do not try to be cheeky and write fake reviews as this can make you spend some nights in jail. Also, you will need to have a real, well designed LinkedIn account to earn from this way.

There are now a few paying websites just for your 5 minutes of software reviews. They don't need to be great reviews, but they want you to connect your LinkedIn with them and need your honest reviews.

First, there is a website called Capterra. Google it and create your user for free, but you cannot go and write random reviews for every software otherwise they won't pay you. Instead, choose relevant software with your current work and start a review on something. The tip here is, do not finish and submit it. Just start a review, maybe write the headline, and close the browser. You can do this for a few software. Now, you will need to wait for a few days. They will e-mail you, asking if you forgot to submit your review, and if you do, they are willing to pay you some money. Follow the link from that e-mail and submit your work. They will then send you selections of how you want the money. You can claim it by Amazon voucher or even by a visa card. Or you can donate the money to some charities which I usually do.

Having an account on Capterra will give you opportunity to have access to a menu that lets you to see some offers which can get you paid if you write a review. There, you will see some software names and costs next to them. They don't need to be a very complex software. Sometimes when I check there, I see they want me to write a review to Microsoft PowerPoint for £10. Easy, isn't it? Or Google Slides or even Zoom. And Capterra might sometimes send you referral links which they ask you to invite people to write reviews and if they do that, you both get paid for some certain amount.

There is another website, called softwarereviews.com and this one only lets you to write 10 reviews. No funny way to try this time but you can create and start writing reviews on your chosen software straight away.

There are some more of similar websites if you google but these two were the only websites that I personally tried and confirmed that they work. You won't earn much, but it is quick and again with zero cost.

Here is one of the examples of outcomes:

13	£15 GBP	Jan 22, 2022	SAP Business ByDesign	Redeem Gift Card

It looks like they asked me to write a review about SAP Business and I did and now I can redeem this as a gift card, which then gives me option to choose between Amazon or visa or donation.

Good luck...

Mystery Shopping, Product Testing and Surveys.

You must have seen lots of ads about winning or earning money on surveys or becoming a mystery shopper. Or even some kind of food or drinks tester. This was very famous when they invited people for e-cigarette testing but the only earning from there was funny moments and travel expenses as well as free e-cigarette trials.

Well, I would say stay away from the surveys but of course it is you who should decide, and it would be good to get an experience from them at some point. Surveys can be fun, but it is like swimming in an ocean without an end. Their promise looks awesome though, they promise ten pounds for a survey but to do that, the survey comes with hundred pages and asks a lot of personal information. Then the other survey never appears, and you see that you can only redeem your money once you reach a certain amount, then all your efforts go into vain. Maybe, if you are lucky, you can earn five pounds in three months by doing these surveys, only if you can find somewhere that pays you as soon as possible. Most of them aren't even tiny, they are all fake. And never ever believe the money maker apps, they are also scam.

On the other hand, mystery shopping is an area where you can do it any time you want, and I tried a few of them years ago. I started with "Roamler", and I think they are the only one with full of active tasks. You can sort them by distance or rewards and do them step by step, following their rules and answering their needs. You only need to take pictures of some shelves in a market and answer their questions like how many tangerines are available or how many bottles of orange juices are looking towards at the customer or similar easy tasks like that. In the end, you get awarded by a few pounds and you claim them into your PayPal.

Be careful about being a mystery shopper though, as it may become dangerous in some circumstances where you are asked to take an inappropriate picture of an entry points of a stock house for example. I happened to get a lot by questions from market security people or even some small shop owners, it was not nice, but you can either tell them you are doing tasks for the vendor, or you can tell them you work for the company that sells the products to the shop. You should only tell them that you are the agent only if you don't have any other options. The best is finding tasks where you go there with written statement from the vendor that you are entitled to do some research on their behalf. These kinds of tasks pay you more but also requires more time.

There used to be a job spotter kind of app which you were taking job ads on shop windows and submitting them online. The payment was nice, you were able to get it any time by vouchers and I remember when I walked a street, I was making twenty pounds for Amazon and spending them without paying delivery fees. I had lots of funny moments though, once I took a "barber required" ad on a barbershop window and the shop owner was outside and he saw me, and I don't know why I couldn't tell him the reason and I had to play some roleplay and told him that I am an experienced barber, I was almost getting employed, it went too far. Sadly, the app has been closed due to pandemic and never got on again...

Upcoming Projects and Investments:

Google Maps Reviews: Reviewing places, uploading pictures, and answering questions.

Reviewing places is now one of my hobbies and even though I don't gain anything yet, I see this as an upcoming project, and I am building up my account and trying to be a famous reviewer.

Anywhere I go, I take pictures and I write a review on Google Maps. And now the Google Maps know me as a local guide and unlocked me some features which gives me the ability to edit a place such as marking it as closed or moved. Not only that, but Google Maps also give you stars, achievements and level points and you gain another feature by levelling up.

Yes, my name on Google Maps is "Yummy Tummy" and this is how my profile looks like now:

Yummy Tummy

Local Guide · Level 7

7,783 points ›

5,000   15,000

Contribute   Reviews   Photos   Edits

And here are my contributions to society as a local guide:

Reviews	366		Ratings	2
Photos	634		Videos	1
Answers	83		Edits	12
Places added	3		Roads added	0
Facts checked	14		Q&A	0
Published lists	0			

Fair enough, isn't it? Some reviews of mine get 1 million views and Google emails me about them. As I said before, there are no actual earnings, but you never know, it may change in future, and I can start getting paid from Google as well.

There had been a few funny things that I may tell you about though. If you give 5 stars to a place, the owner usually replies to you and says their thanks. But if you give them 1 or 2 stars, they sometimes reply with a phone number to discuss what was wrong about your visit. Some of them are really trying to make it up, and one time, on a poor pub visit, I was offered free drinks a few times just for my bad review. They apologised and we became good friends after having some drinks and chat. They are all human after all. There was another place that offered me free snacks and free products too to change my review which I refused. There are so many different stuffs to see when you do such things as a hobby and in other words when you have time to do such things...

Another point of this was also again creating memories... I am living inside of my memories as you know so this is an important part of my work. Now the Google has my own pictures, and they will be there forever. Aren't we all made of memories in the end, basically? That's why I love spreading good memories anywhere possible such as a review with a coffee in my hand. Then years later when I check a place, I will see my picture there from years ago... This is the main reason actually for almost anything I do... We are made of memories, and we will remain in memories. All it matters is having them in quality and having great memories, as every second is precious when you are with your loved ones, and you need to make it count when casting these memories.

Here in this screenshot, you can see that my pictures on Google Maps achieved a score of 2 million views. Even though I don't get paid, as I said before, I am doing this for fun. Who knows? There might be an opportunity to get something in return but again, as I said before, I am doing this for memories and will keep doing this...

A lot of people are seeing your photos on Google Maps!
Google
2,000,000
Hi Yummy,
2,000,000 views! You're a top photographer on Google Maps
You've just accomplished what very few people have done: reached 2,000,000 photo views! Keep it up!
Yi Fang Brac...   21/10/2022
619
iRepair   28/10/2022
448
Oodles Slo...
436
Market Inn ...
369
Trunkwell H...
164
Ranelagh School
Map data ©2022

Not only that, but I can also create places on Google Maps and publish them because of my grade. I can edit and amend details of places too. It gets funnier and interesting in each grade. Just enjoy, and good luck...

More Upcoming Projects and Investments:

Amazon Item Reviews: Writing reviews for items.

Again, another reviewing project and this one is a bit more work related as if you want to be an official Amazon reviewer, you really need to write good and long reviews about certain categories. After this, Amazon might accept you into its "Vine" community and you can get paid or can get free items and so.

I haven't felt ready to go into this path yet because this is not a passive income and needs serious work. Why would I write such long reviews, I would write a book instead or write an article? But if you want to progress on this path, why not?

There had been fun activities on Amazon too that you might want to hear. Again, I wrote my real feelings about an item that I bought, and it didn't make the seller happy, so they contacted me for free products in the exchange of changing my rate and review, which I again declined. It might be the other way around, too much to explore in this area.

There is a fun fact about Amazon which might not be true but it is on social media so I don't see any reason why I shouldn't talk about it... Well, what happened is, a small business created their own store and began to sell camera tripods on Amazon. It reached 3 million dollars in sales which was about 0.0001% of Amazon's revenue. Then

Amazon copied the tripods as exactly and sold them as Amazon Basics Tripods and then they banned the small tripod company from Amazon. This could be all fake though, but could also be true, which I would believe because if you google Amazon tripod ban, you will get hundreds of news about it… Anyway, we still all love Amazon and how it works, and we still shop there, and my book is on Amazon so enough chit-chat… They made some things easier for us, that's right, they have an excellent customer service. Do you know why bookstores don't like Amazon? Same reason as why banks don't like crypto and the same reason that why taxis don't like Uber. I can make this longer, cinemas don't like Netflix, and hotels don't like Airbnb… Also, another one coming from pandemic that 9-5's doesn't like remote work. And why? Because innovation is often disliked. This is the only simple answer.

This reviewing for items or anything could be done on other platforms too such as eBay but do consider that, it is quality reviews that separates you from others, not quantity…

What I did with the money?
Before I start...

You must know how to spend your money well, otherwise you are poor. This is the summary. If your lifestyle does depend on money, you are poor, no matter how much you got, you would still be poor. Sorry about that but it all depends on how you live and how you want to live.

There is a common story about a rich man and his driver. If you haven't heard, let me tell you: One day the rich man dies, and the driver gets married with his ex-wife. So, everything inherited to the driver and the driver said: "I always thought I was working for him, but I see that he was working for me..."

Every day and every moment are precious, and you need to make the most of them. Especially with the loved ones.

If you are choosing the cheapest product but you desire the better which you can afford, I can tell that you are always waiting the perfect moment to be happy and waiting things to settle, which means you are not living the moment, and wasting your life. Just look at yourself and see what you were doing about 10 years ago, is it full of happiness and satisfaction or is it full of regret? Your life may end suddenly, all the money you saved for later could be gone in seconds. Time is the greatest richness, and I am not expecting anyone very young to understand these values, as you get wisdom in time.

We desire for things that we do not have... Once we got them, we lose its attention, or we only understand its value after we lose it. This is about being a human and how we are made. A better person should have a great character as all can agree. Do everything but do not lose your character, or even adapt or change on the circumstances, always keep your personality, and character and keep it strong. Believe me, nobody will remember your salary, or how busy you were, or how many hours you worked or how many quality bags or clothes you owned. But they will all remember how you made them feel, and if you kept your word or if they could count on you and the time you spent with them.

I know you are still expecting the answer to the question of what I did with the money, but I am getting to the point and trying to give you the whole picture before I start of what I did and what I have been doing.

Let me get this straight, I am not a filthy rich and I have never wanted to be one of them or even approach the level of them. My understanding of being rich is different. I hope I can let you understand my mindset and how I approach things in different way. Did you know, if the given information was correct, the world's billionaires aka the filthy rich got richer by 3.9 trillion dollars during the pandemic while worker class lost 3.7 trillion dollars in earnings? And do you remember the news about this? They said the pandemic is affecting the mental health of the rich more than the poor. This is disgusting, isn't it? This is why I have never wanted to be that much rich and no intention to become one. And also, I can't be one of them even if I wanted to!

People say one of your feet is in the mud if your only income is your salary. I agree with this however working is essential, and you are right about thinking of how you have to work to make money to afford to live on a planet that you didn't even ask to be on. Do you know what they say about the earning relationship of a boss and their worker? They say, the boss makes a dollar, while the worker makes a dime. Basically true, but technically an average CEO makes 265 times the average wage of a worker, so a boss makes 26.50 dollar, while the worker makes a dime. This also sheds light to the description of minimum wage, an employer who pays the minimum wage is basically saying that they would pay any less only if they could! Sometimes everything you see is not true, they are fine until you do some research, but when you start to see the whole picture, you lose your faith to humanity and ambition to anything. Ignorance is bliss, I completely agree to that, because if you don't know about the problem, the life can be very peaceful...

While we are talking about the pandemic and aftereffects, remember when they said that we are in the same boat. This was complete rubbish, we were not in the same boat, we were in the same storm. While some people had bigger boats, some of us had smaller boats. We couldn't survive the pandemic; we have been destroyed. This is what I always say, maybe we died during the pandemic, but we just don't know it yet... And what have we learnt from the pandemic? We learnt that the life is short, all jobs are temporary, health is wealth and always save money. We also learnt that majority of people can comfortable and efficiently work from home and remember how funny that every employer implemented the home office working style in a few days! If there hadn't been the pandemic, some companies would still have been constantly complaining about working from home schemes. We also have seen that rich people are in fact less immune than the poor. Life just doesn't get easier, you get stronger. Do you know the pattern of times versus men? Hard times create strong men pattern? Follows by strong men create good times and good times create weak men. We are now at the stage where weak men create hard times...

Life is short, and by the age of 30, you should have a few bucks in your bank account, a few bad relationship stories, anxiety, and back pain. Don't worry, this is normal, you should worry if you don't have them. But don't think that you are smarter than the previous generations. Just about 40 or 50 years ago, the owner's manual of a car shows you how to adjust the valves, and today it warns you not to drink the contents of the battery. Yes, this is how we evolved. When the energy prices increased, I checked the citizens advise website, searched some tips on how to save energy, do you know what was the first advise they give? They said, close the doors or windows. I immediately closed the web page. We are definitely living in a time where intelligent people are being silenced so that the stupid people won't be offended. Just remember the old cartoons. They were very fun, and no one was racist or anything like that. How come we changed this fast in a very funny way? There is another saying, and I believe it was in one of Dostoyevsky's books, he said that the tolerance will reach such a level that intelligent people will be banned from thinking so as not to offend the imbeciles. Well, this is a little bit harsher but truer than what I tried to summarise, isn't it? This is true and if you think I am whining, I am not, there is no solution to this and like people say, I agree that every day we stray away from God. Sometimes we just don't need a solution, we only want to be mad...

The root cause of this generation's problem of today is basically not listening to each other, in other words having no empathy. Have you also seen this that they talk for an hour but when you start talking, they just don't listen, or you won't even get a question from them? This reminds me the two people arguing on which drawing is correct on the floor. There is a 6 or 9 written on the floor which you must have seen it before and one of them is saying six, and another one is saying nine. And usually, the moral of this drawing says that just because you are right, doesn't mean, I am wrong. Well, again basically true, but technically one of those people is wrong. Because someone painted a six or a nine on the floor! It is that simple! They need to orient themselves by backing up their arguments, see if there are any other numbers to align with, as an instance. Maybe there is another factor that could reveal the possibility of truth, but they don't care. No one wants to listen to each other; they don't do any research; they just want to be right. Sometimes they yell you each other, I would always say, raise your argument, not your voice. And I hate to see people yelling at people...

The world has turned into a clown world, there is nothing I can disagree with that but sadly accept it. There is a certain movie about a mentally ill clown, and by watching it many times, I came to a point that some things cannot be unseen. As people say, each day we stray away from God. And you must have also heard from old people that, this is the end of the world. This is mostly because now we can have all the news about everyone or everything and what's going on easily. Before that, people were still the same, the only difference is now the information that we can get from them. This still doesn't change the fact that the world is a clown world. Once you get yourself out of the slaving system, you find your inner-self and then inner-peace. You get time to think and get time to do whatever makes you happy. There are some small life hacks that I should mention about, for example, are you overthinking, then you should write something. Or are you feeling burnt out, then you need to read something. Are you sad, then you need exercise or are you anxious, do some meditation? The list goes on, are you angry, you need to listen to music or are you stressed, you need to go out for a walk. These are very simple life hacks that we forget, or we neglect easily. Last one, are you lazy or getting lazier, reduce screen time...

I have been a lazy person time to time and because of this, I usually became the solution maker. Because lazy people create solutions to overcome problems. Some companies prefer lazy people over clever ones, because while clever employers work like a machine, lazy ones create automation so that they can have free time to themselves. I am not saying being clever is not good, I am saying it is all about your choices... If you choose to be a sheep, you will find lots of herders. On the other hand, if you want to be free, you need to work on it. The time between the first moment of your job and the last moment of your job is your life. This is about any job, any work, any study, or anything that you do... I am not talking about a lifetime job; I am talking about making your moments liveable. It is again what you choose and your priorities. Sometimes they would ask you if you were result oriented, and believe me, this is one of the words that I hate the most. Being a result oriented in a project in a job is okay but being a result oriented in life makes your life miserable. You need to enjoy every moment with yourself or with your loved ones when doing something. It could be building a chair, painting something, even cooking or making a puzzle. Result is not the one you need to achieve; it is the path. They asked to someone, what was the best thing of your journey, and someone replied, it was the company... Believe me, if you are result oriented in life, you will find yourself alone and unhappy with your phone in your hand...

Now, let me tell you a joke... One day an infinite number of mathematicians walk into a bar and the first one orders a beer. The second one orders half a beer. The third one order a quarter of a beer. But then the bartender says you are all idiots and pours two beers. It is that simple, the joke is as same as the joke when the ATM charges you £2 to get your own money and then tells you to cover your PIN so you don't get robbed... Simple isn't it? Be smart, be innovative, be knowledgeable, do not be result oriented in life and do not waste your precious moments, these are the key elements.

Considering today's problems, you should be thinking that maybe not everything is simple. It is only because nobody trusts anybody these days and they are hundred percent right for doing this. When people see something that looks too good to be true, they don't believe it. Especially when you see something free, your first instinct tells you that it is fake. It could be fake though, you know what they say, if a product is free, you are the product. It could be an advertisement too but still you might need to learn everything about it and read the terms and conditions before you accept it. I am telling you this because once I saw something about a free product, then found out that consenting to one free product automatically enrols you into the advantage program which has some monthly fee with and additional activation fee upon initial enrolment and some cancellation fee if you decide to cancel it. This is non-sense, but it is true and as again, people have all the right not to believe and trust each other nowadays...

When you see something that tells you to try it for free then asks your credit card details, you should stop there. Let me give you some advice on the latest trends of corporate language and their translations. Firstly, terms and conditions mean there is no refund policy and the privacy policy that you hear a lot is simply a data mining agreement. Cookies on the other hand that you accept to keep them in your phone or computer are spyware acceptance. And if you want to read a blog or a simple essay, for example ten awesome tips to change your life, you will find yourself in suicide by ads overdose. And do you know why sometimes we do the traffic signs captchas to check if we are human, this is to train their artificial intelligence for free... Many of them to be learnt and we need to be adapting. I really want to tell you something that I saw about confusing artificial intelligence, someone was advising people that we should confuse the system by searching opposites, such as ice and fire, black and white, calming music and metal music, or swimming and hiking, believe me these searches would not confuse the system but make it better trained and would improve it. Sometimes it is so funny watching people trying to declare war on artificial intelligence. Too much sci-fi movies I presume?

Everyone need to be tolerant these days but let me say that being tolerant means being willing to tolerate stuff, it doesn't mean blindly accepting anything thrown at you. Keep your dignity and stay strong. I know the government is eyeing your minimum wage income when collecting taxes instead of looking at billionaires, huge corporations and even politicians. And when you start earning something, the government say it is our gain, but if you lose something, it is your loss. Those huge corporations that I mentioned is feeding the filthy rich in a way that you cannot imagine.

Now, let me tell you that if every person on earth just recycled everything, stopped using plastic straws, and drove electric cars, just a hundred of those huge corporations would still produce more than 70% of total global emission... And let me get this straight with an example that we all live, you go to a grocery store and buy some loaf of bread in a plastic bag and a gallon of milk in a plastic jug, and a pack of napkins in a plastic wrap, a plastic bottle of ketchup or a supermarket brand salad in a plastic tub and some sliced meat or fish in a plastic bag, and then you go to the tills and they won't give you a plastic bag to carry them to home, or they charge you extra, because the plastic bag is bad for the environment. And not every plastic item is recyclable, have you noticed that? Just look at the packaging, most of them will say "not yet recycled" or "do not recycle at home" … I do also remember that decades ago, people would say, plastic was the only solution for a better environment to reduce cutting trees to create paper… Clown world!

This is what they are, isn't it? They first create a problem and then sell the solution. The idiots are always around so they get well fed by them. The bosses of huge corporations or whatever you say, CEO or anything like that, they always get themselves the best and then tell the middle class to support the minorities. And even then, still make us feel bad about not doing anything as a middle class. You must have seen the equality versus justice drawing where people are using crates to watch a match, and my opinion on this is, when I first saw it, I said this is crime, because they are watching the match without tickets… On the other hand, equity or equality shouldn't be pursued, equity means, equality of outcome, not equality of opportunity. Equality of outcome basically means, no matter what you do, you will get the same results in the end, imagine you spend the day working and you get hundred pounds for your work, and some random guy decides to chill at home, and he also gets hundred pounds, this is the equality of outcome… Karl Marx once said, if you decided to hang the capitalists, a capitalist would see you the rope. Same as the pandemic, when they said the world is ending, people were asking if they need a logo...

We do not take everything serious and maybe we are doing it right, otherwise everything becomes a problem and anxiety kicks in, especially at nights... You should have positive thoughts and vibes and don't forget that most of the times, your brain, your mind is your biggest enemy. I completely agree that because sometimes my brain makes up things that never happened or never going to happen and makes me awake during nights... Alcohol is not the solution for this but meditation and yoga. However, the root cause is the random and temporary people around you. You need to be picky when you want to spend time with them. Sometimes you meet someone, and you know from the first moment that you want to spend your whole life without them. Be with friends that you would really call them as a friend. Otherwise, the path leads to anxiety and maybe more...

What Have We Learnt So Far?

By now, you should have got the whole idea of being rich and the tips of how to become one.

But really, what have we learnt?

Again, we are living in a farm called the world and we are all sheep, there are some farmers which are the filthy rich and we are being farmed by them so they can live their life. In other words, we are all slaves. They would sell the air to us if they could. Do you think they care for us? Of course, they don't, they only care about themselves. They would only care if you cannot work for them! We can only be better sheep or in other words a better slave by guaranteeing our future and I showed you the path. It is all up to you now, you either choose one of the paths or you become a hater and a loser.

What else we learnt? We learnt that you do not earn or have money suddenly like by a lottery. I don't believe they exist anyway, but I shouldn't comment about it because I know most of the money that has spent on lottery goes to charities. And people buy hopes by playing lottery. Imagine I wrote a book like this, how did I get rich, by lottery and what did I do with it, ate it, or lost it. A book with one or two sentences. Really? Just google a probability calculator for a six balls lottery, the odds are usually about one in ten million. And the probability exists only if the lottery is legit. But again, they use the money on charities so yes, you can play and buy hopes.

Let me mention this again that those paths that I showed you were all tried by me. All works, however, those were tried starting from year 2017 until 2023. So, consider this too, because everything is changing, and rich people do not want poor to become better than anyone, so the system is adapting to them. Do not forget that, and do not lose hope. They want you to fail, don't feed them.

If any system you tried fails, do not give up. Instead, learn from mistakes. Do not be a hater, instead think positive and become a lover.

More importantly, spend everything with your loved ones. As again, if you are not spending two or three pounds for a Latte, you are poor. Those tiny savings will never make you rich and those shouldn't be counted as savings in the first place. Make sure you are making every moment the most.

Last of all, if by any chance, any filthy rich reads this, I want to ask, why and why? You had every opportunity to use your money on good, making the world a liveable space for every other human, but you didn't. Just asking, why? I am asking this to them, what did you do with the money?

I will tell you what I did with the money...

What Haven't We Learnt So Far?

Now that you are coming to the end, and I want you to think that or imagine that you have unlimited money. Think about it, or you have plenty of it, or everything you want to buy is free, completely free. Food, dress, cars, houses, everything is free, or you have the whole cash in the world. Think about it and tell me what you would do with the money or with the freedom...

Did you think I was teaching you how to earn the money with this book? No, I was only teaching you how to spend the money, or what to do with the money. (Not in an investment way as you have already seen.)

Now, for your answer, if you chose to buy houses, because they are all free, or chose to buy all the cars, or items or anything that you can stack up, then you have learnt nothing so far. Not only that, if you really chose to get yourself hundreds of houses or expensive and valuable items, collections, and anything like that, nothing would make you happy and this selection would stamp you as a slave which would never change. Sorry for the facts but this is true.

If salary or money is your only thought and only criteria when deciding or doing something, or moving to somewhere, or even relocating, and you are not considering anything else other than the income, sorry again but nothing can take you out of the slavery. Being slave to money is not curable even if you have the endless amount of it.

Now again think about it, what would you do if you had endless money? The answer is the same: Loved ones... You should spend your money with loved ones and make the most of it! It is this simple!

So, enough talk and philosophy... Now that you got the idea of who I am and what possible I would do, you must be guessing that I did fine with the money. Yes, that's right, as I said before, I am not a big spender, maybe I don't know how to spend it or maybe I know. Or maybe I know how to save and keep the money. Who knows? The truth is, I never overspent and never lost anything. I didn't gamble, didn't spend it on something that is a complete waste and didn't give it away...

I built the system, I maintained enough to cover my expenses, I assured my family can manage without working for a lifetime and got enough savings to give them the life that they deserve.

I didn't buy hundreds of houses as I believe even a single house would cause more headaches than joy. I only bought the best house in the UK for my family and designed it with the best equipment and built a happy environment. I didn't buy the most expensive car but bought the one that would make me the happiest.

I created several bank accounts in different banks and put enough money to cover a few years of expenses in each of them and marked them as savings accounts. I am still adding into them, donating some to charities and trying to create a better living for whoever needs it, helping animal rescues and giving them enough to build shelters. This is making me a better human and these kinds of activities are separating me from the filthy rich.

I chose having to know that there is enough money to cover anything that would stop me from living my dream over having unlimited houses or farms or whatever assets. I believed that wealth comes from happiness and being peaceful, not from properties or piles.

I kept my job but instead of working for a boss, I chose to work for the community to make a better world. I believe I did my part in this world, even though it is small work, it is honest work, at least I tried.

I always wanted to buy things from any market without looking at the price labels or discounts or any deals, and I managed to achieve that, and then I figured out that some supermarket brands are better than the pricey items and mostly the cheapest products make me happier than the most expensive ones. Of course, at first, I did mistakes, I bought every new product that I saw, every chocolate, every drink, every sweet, and anything you can imagine. Did those make me happy? No, I got fat! I had to work a lot to lose that fat! Now I am trying to stay away from such things.

I explored everywhere possible with my family and stored great memories. I didn't choose the expensive restaurants but chose the ones that would make me and my family happy. Mostly, the cheapest burger is way more delicious than a gourmet burger.

I am sorry if I got you frustrated now by letting you know that I didn't lose it by gambling, or crypto… No, I always tread firmly on the ground and have never been a witless man. I reached a certain level of wisdom, and I am proud of that. I didn't earn them suddenly and I started from scratch. I wasn't lucky but I was smart...

To get them, I agree that the level of richness needs to reach to a certain level and the soul should be satiated by tasting, experiencing, and maybe having everything. After that, the person understands what makes them happy and what makes them joyless. It is not the money that brings happiness, it is you and your choices.

Now that you learnt how I got rich and the ways that how I became one. So, what is stopping you now? All you need is to choose a path that suits you the best and carry on with it. Very simple, decide and build your system and then you can relax and after some time your only worry would be what to do with the money... This answer is also simple, don't forget these two words: Loved ones. Because without them, we are nothing, and meaningless.

My last and only word is money should be spent for loved ones and the life should be spent with them.

Good luck...

www.ingramcontent.com/pod-product-compliance
Lightning Source LLC
Chambersburg PA
CBHW031308250726

48656CB00005B/1702